5X More Freedom and Growth

How to Leverage Your Team and Work Less

Jon L. Myers , CFP®, MBA, ChFC®, CLTC, CASL®

5X More Freedom and Growth

Published by:
90-Minute Books
Newinformation Inc
302 Martinique Drive
Winter Haven, FL 33884
www.90minutebooks.com

ISBN-13: 978-0692419243
ISBN-10: 0692419241

For more information on 90-Minute Books including finding out how you can publish your own lead generating book, visit www.90minutebook.com or call (863) 318-0464

Here's What's Inside

Vestal, NY
April 2015

One of the things people often ask me is how I'm able to run such a growing and profitable business without working more and more. We've all heard the adage 'work smarter, not harder.' What does that mean exactly? I've been in the financial services business for 22 years. It wasn't until the last five years that I really started applying the strategies I'm going to share with you today, that my business really took off.

These are strategies that I've been sharing with financial advisors one on one and the reason I wanted to write this book.

Helping financial advisors get out of their own way and really grow their practice is what I'm passionate about. I've seen what works and what can be a recipe for burnout.

What follows is the transcript where I share with you strategies I've used to grow my business 6 X in five years.

I hope this book educates you and helps change your way of thinking about growing your financial services business and encourages you to build a team that will give you the freedom you desire.

Enjoy the Book!

Jon Myers

5X More Freedom and Growth!

Susan: Good afternoon, this is Susan Austin and I'm super excited to be here with Jon Myers. Jon is going to be sharing with us his thoughts and ideas on how financial advisor teams can work less, but in fact, earn more. Welcome Jon.

Jon: Thank you Susan. Glad to be here.

Susan: Why did you want to write a book on how to achieve more in less time, Jon?

Jon: Actually I didn't at first. I was pushed by team members to write a book because of all the knowledge I've gained over the years building successful teams. I finally agreed and thought it would be a great way to share my thoughts with others.

Susan: You're going to share with us today how financial advisors can earn five times more but work less. I'll admit I'm a little skeptical Jon. Those two things don't normally go hand in hand.

Jon: That's okay. How can I make a statement like 'you can earn five times more money and work less time' without some skepticism?

Susan: Yes, we'd like to know the answer to that.

Jon: My first thought is to run my business as if I was suddenly not here tomorrow. With that in mind I need to do two key activities: delegation and empowerment. Delegation leads to empowerment and empowerment leads to capability. My team is always moving up market having more opportunity to do what makes them passionate. This leads to capability.

Susan: Do you find that a lot of the finance people you are talking about are hesitant to build a team around them? Do they feel they are the face and brand of the company so it's hard for them to delegate? The buck stops with them, so to speak.

Jon: Yes, in fact, I had some of these fears when I was looking to grow my business. I was not immune to them. However, I've grown my business six times in the last five years and the reason is because I've worked through some of these fears. I let go of some of the things that I thought I wouldn't be able to let go of. I learned to work on my business, not in it. You have to give up pieces along the way and build your team around you. This is a marathon, not a sprint. I don't try to accomplish everything at once, but keep it going. It's about my team and I'm just one of many faces the clients interact with. My clients depend on my team and the business is healthy because of it.

Susan: If you don't learn to delegate then you have to be involved in every client conversation, every presentation and you won't be able to grow as there is only one you, right? You can't leverage if you don't bring in a bigger team.

Jon: Correct. It's incredibly inefficient to be in every meeting. At first I felt guilty about it. When clients came in I told them, "You are meeting with my staff today, but I'm going to be right across the hall, if you have any questions I'll come in." I would make sure that I greeted them and had some connection because these are people I'd been working with 10, 15, 20 years. However, I continue to meet with clients two out of four meetings per year.

Susan: Very good. So you still meet with clients?

Jon: Yes, I see about six clients a week.

Susan: How many clients would you have seen before you learned to delegate more?

Jon: Previously I saw 12 to 15 clients a week. Now I see fewer clients, work 25 hours per week, and spend half my time doing strategic business planning.

Why More Advisors Don't Delegate

Susan: Why are some advisors reluctant to rely on their team more, Jon?

Jon: A lot of advisors will worry that their team is not experienced enough or that they won't be able to work with the client in quite the same way and they're worried the clients are going to be unhappy. These are common fears.

Often times you may feel you can do the job better than the people who work for you, but that's just not true. For example, when I made the decision I wanted other advisors to do my client meetings, we implemented a process. First I demonstrated to the advisor by having him sit in on a client meeting.

Next, the advisor did role playing with me. Then the advisor did the meeting with the client with me present. And finally, I let him do it on his own with the client. It might take six months of my being in the meeting with the advisor, it might take a year, but that's how you mitigate the fear that your team isn't as good as you are. You have to be brave. You have to plan it and think about it. You can't just wing it and turn it over. There needs to be a process of transition.

Susan: Why did you do this? If you were happy working only 25, 30 hours a week, what was your impetus to want to make these changes?

Jon: Five years ago I was in the top 10% of advisors with my firm. Now, as a result of these changes, I'm in the top 1%. Five years ago I was making a really good living. I had four people working for me and I could have done that for the rest of my life. But then I started thinking I wanted to be more challenged. At that same time, I had an advisor come to me who wanted me to buy his business. I wasn't that interested at first but then I decided to pursue it and within one year I increased my practice sales from $600,000 to $1,000,000. It was a very smooth process and this got me on the path of doing recruitment and acquisition. Today I am doing $2.7m in sales.

Don't Focus on Managing, Focus on Leading

Susan: Do you find a lot of advisors don't want to be managers? They don't want to deal with all the people problems. They just want to meet with the clients.

Jon: That's very true. In fact, I'm more of a leader than a manager. I work on my practice, not in it. I have three advisors who have management responsibility inside the business along with servicing 250 clients each.

My managers are very different from normal staff. This is true because they are required to have entrepreneurial thinking so they can manage the different phases of my business. Therefore, I'm not managing personnel problems at all. I give advice and I help out if needed, but they do the heavy lifting.

Susan: I think that would be a big fear that growing your team means growing your problems.

Jon: You do have more problems, but they are different problems. You solve them through leadership. If you want to grow your business you have to learn very clearly the distinction between working on your practice and working in it. Managers work in the business, leaders work on the business.

How to Build Your Team

Susan: Let's talk about your steps for the advisors getting to five times more freedom and growth.

Jon: We'll start with team building. Team building is about empowering people. It's building around your team's strengths. I don't want to manage people's weaknesses. Rather, I want to lead them to work within their strengths. We are looking for people who are driven, hardworking and passionate, and want to grow. Everybody can say they want to grow, but you have to have the behavior that goes along with it.

Also, it has to do with being very relationship driven and going very deep with my team and very deep with clients: building strong relationships. Those relationships can have a tremendous impact on building a practice because there's a lot of loyalty and commitment that comes with it.

Susan: Because you are working with fewer clients I assume you have to do more dollar volume with those clients to make up the difference. Is that a fair assumption?

Jon: Yes, but you have to have very efficient systems to manage the volume. I spend just 15 minutes of preparation for any one of my meetings. Each meeting has a different agenda and those agendas are defined in advance and we track all action items.

Susan: Some advisors meet with 40 clients a week and you only meet with six. Does that mean you have to make 200% more from each client to offset the volume difference?

Jon: No, it means my advisor team meets with 50 clients per week. We have 1,100 clients. We still have to service every one of them. I talk about relationships with clients but we can still do high volume because I have a team of advisors meeting with all those clients. It's the team that makes all the difference.

Susan: It's not all dependent on Jon.

Jon: Exactly. Some advisors may find it hard to step away. The advisors want to know "How do I tell my clients that I am not going to be in all the meetings going forward?" I didn't tell them that. I made a conscious decision to not tell them. I gradually stepped out of meetings and it worked out. However, I'm always going to be available to my clients.

Susan: You don't have to put out a memo announcing that you aren't going to be in the meetings.

Jon: It's a process that unfolded over a year. I did it very carefully and I did it differently with each client.

Susan: So you are looking for someone who can do more than just sell, I imagine?

Jon: Correct and that's why we use specific conative aptitude testing. Part of building my team is to know how to find different strengths which help to offset different weaknesses. Wherever there is a weakness in our team, we make hiring decisions that allow us to pick and choose the right people who will maximize productivity.

This has been an evolving process. If we are talking two years ago I don't think I would have had the clarity and vision that I have right now to discuss this. I was going through the process of really changing the direction of where the business was going, and this book is helping me document the process we undertook.

When we buy practices, for example, we will look at five and choose two. I'm not going to buy five. I'm going to choose just two. I'm going to be very selective that the practices really fit into our culture and match up with the team. We have to go really deep with each acquisition and make sure they are a fit for our modeling.

Susan: Do you mind sharing some of the criteria you use for hiring advisors?

Jon: You have to be careful that they fit into your culture really well. You have to treat each advisor somewhat differently. It doesn't mean you rule out working with someone from a different culture, but you have to figure out if somebody is really passionate, loyal, and open-minded at their job. If they've got experience you can probably find a way they can be a great team player even if the culture is quite different. We're going to create *our* culture. That's what's going to work. It isn't going to be mine. It isn't going to be theirs. It's going to be ours. It's people who fit the modeling and the modeling is ever-changing.

Susan: Humans are pretty complex. Is it hard to do?

Jon: That's where I'm most creative. I figure it out as I go and that's part of my passion and unique ability. I don't know how teachable that is, but that's one of the reasons I'm doing the book. I'm hoping this is going to help me provide some real clarity when I talk to and recruit advisors.

Susan: Let's look at this. What do you personally look for when you talk with advisors?

Jon: One big thing is loyalty. Another is having a good work ethic. Another attribute we look for is drive. Drive is very important. We also look for them to be passionate.

We also are very careful and diligent about letting go of people. It's very important to let go of people who are pulling the team down.

Susan: I read somewhere recently that companies will keep a bad hire on board 18 months longer than they should.

Jon: That's the nature of people. You get into denial. You get into hope. You get into all these different things and it's just inefficient and, truthfully, it's not good for the person, the team, or you.

How to Network for Recruitment and Acquisition

Susan: Let's talk about recruitment and acquisition because I would imagine if someone is going to build a team they have to recruit and acquire. I would love to hear how you approach recruitment and acquisition.

Jon: There was an advisor in my area who wanted me to buy his practice, but I didn't want to at the time. So in the end I decided to buy his practice and this had a tremendous impact on me in building my team. Now I'm passionate about buying practices.

Sometimes the best thing you can do as an entrepreneur is buy the practice without the team being totally in place. You do have to have enough infrastructure to do the job and then look at building the team as you go. You have to let the opportunity, to some extent, drive your building of a team. That's hard for a lot of advisors. They think that they have to have the team in place before they buy a practice, but without the practice how do you grow your team?

You've got to be very careful not to grow too fast and at the same time to keep it going. If you are not moving forward you are moving backwards. To me this is about progress, not perfection.

There is a lot of competition with acquisitions. I've done pretty well with them. I've bought four practices in the last five years. I owe it to our focus on building advisor relationships and networking.

For advisors who are selling practices it's really about two things. It's asking: after the sale of the business, are they going to be okay and are their clients going to be taken care of? You have to develop a relationship and go very deep with an advisor to make sure what you bring to the table is going to match their needs.

How to Do 20 Years of Marketing in 5 Years' Time

Jon: I've been able to grow my business six times in five years. The way I was able to do that was by buying multiple practices. You could spend 20 years asking for referrals and doing seminars or you can grow your business exponentially by buying a practice. Just one such purchase can be equivalent to 20 years of marketing.

Susan: It's another way to leverage growth. You can go out and build the business by yourself but why not skip ahead and acquire it?

Jon: Yes. There are opportunities out there. All advisors have relationships with other advisors. Everybody has a chance to grow through acquisition, but they need to network and build capacity to make it happen.

The other piece to this is recruitment. I fell into recruitment. I thought, "That's interesting. I can recruit other advisors, maybe even those who might be making a quarter million dollars a year in revenue, and bring them into my team and have them work for me." I'm franchising the franchise, if you will.

We've recruited four people. One of them is in her late 60s. She sold her practice to me, but she's managing the practice. She's really enjoying semi-retirement. It's profitable and I own equity. This is ideal for both parties.

It's an interesting concept to have her take care of her clients. She's still working, she's got her retirement in place, and she's making a nice income. She will probably retire in three or four years. I'm building advisor readiness, if you will, with my team to be able to take over her business once she leaves. That's recruitment.

Susan: If you are an advisor who has been relying solely on getting your name out into the marketplace, this is a whole other level to growing your business considerably.

Jon: Yes, I was told by other people that I'll never be able to do what I've done. When I do my networking I tell them right up front. We may not be a match. I'm not trying to convince you of anything. If you don't want to come with me, that's okay because I want people to want to be part of this process, 100% in. This process could take six months or three years. It needs to be well thought out.

Susan: This isn't a get rich quick approach here. You are very leery about who you bring onto your team.

Jon: Absolutely, and I'm really passionate about that. It's not about money at all. It's about having an impact on people.

In fact, I'm pretty tough in negotiating; however, I will pay a premium for a practice. If it's a really good practice I'll pay 20 percent more than the market because the break over point is probably six months later. Usually these things pay for themselves in two to three years. But I want to be fair to both sides. I don't just pay premiums without thinking this practice will be a really good practice for the modeling.

Susan: Interesting. When you said you were 'tough in negotiation' I wasn't expecting you to go the way you went. I thought you were going to talk about how you get it for 20% less not 20% more.

Jon: I don't do that at all. I pay a premium, but it's got to be a premium practice.

How to Build the Infrastructure

Susan: I like it. Let's talk about the infrastructure someone is going to need to support the practice.

Jon: I have a young team. I have 14 people; four who are between the ages of 25 and 28. Two out of the three people on my management team are young people. They've been in the business for five to six years. They do my hiring and firing, but I tell them, "I'm going to put you out on the trapeze. You are going to have all kinds of opportunities and I'm going to be the safety net."

Again, I'm working on my business and not in it. It allows them to really develop and grow. Teach your staff and trust them. You've got to lead. If you don't know how to do it, find somebody who does. Find whatever your weaknesses are and fill them with strengths.

Susan: It's interesting because I'm getting from just discussing with you that having the right team is a passion.

Jon: Yes. I love leading teams. I enjoy being connected with everybody on my team. I have locations across upstate New York and I'm connected with them all in different ways. This is very important.

We have a weekly meeting on Thursday for an hour and a half. Each member of the management team has five projects that get completed and updated every quarter; we track them in this meeting. It helps a lot for where we are going in the business that each person has their own five projects that they are working on.

The four of us track these 20 projects on one sheet. I didn't want to have more than 20 because it's inefficient. For us, if we are going to bring in a new project, something else has to be eliminated. It keeps us really efficient.

Susan: Right and make sure these are right projects.

Jon: That's right.

Susan: Are there other systems?

Jon: There is a system for how we service clients and how we manage human resources. We systematize processes and we are always looking at trying to make things have better flow. We have job descriptions for each person and we are always making sure that the jobs are being done most efficiently. We are always developing our people and paying them well.

Susan: I totally got the glimpse of the picture of your marketing/growing the business system but just to highlight a couple other places where an advisor may not even think to put a system in place.

Jon: Having an infrastructure is really about my team. You are right. The team building and the networking for recruitment and acquisition is what I do all the time, but the infrastructure is developed by my management team. The managers do it. They have great instincts and do a great job. I stay out of it except for overseeing.

For example, let's review our client service modeling. We put together a coding system for when we see each client while defining the purpose for each meeting. This helps to identify the agenda ahead of time. Having a code identified for each meeting means everyone knows exactly what their job is, without being told. Also, we can easily identify where each client is in their annual meeting cycle, creating consistency in the client experience. It's very efficient.

Susan: Right because people would be running around in circles trying to figure for the Johnson meeting at 3:00 o'clock.

Jon: Before this I was preparing for all meetings. I spent a whole day preparing for meetings for the next three to four days and it was very inefficient. A lot of advisors do it that way and now if you go into our office you will not think it's busy. People are relaxed. There's laughter. One of our core values is enjoyment/harmony and it's probably the top core value. I want people to have fun at work and that has to do with them knowing their systems and jobs. They know what has to be done and they are improving all the time.

Also, it's really good for the client because they know what to expect.

It also lowers stress ... this goes without saying: lowering stress for the advisor and for the team. One of our advisor recruits that we brought on was very attracted to us because of our systems which meant that he'd be able to do more in less time. His reason for wanting to be part of the team was just what the title of the book is: more freedom while working less.

I feel very strong about this. I don't want anybody working more than 40 hours a week. I don't want people working harder; I want them working more efficiently. If they can get the job done in less time I'm happy.

Susan: Someone that's looking to just acquire a practice, just to dump on more work without the proper systems and procedures in place, is going to have chaos.

Jon: Absolutely. One of the reasons we have much better systems is that we hired a consultant to help us. Don't be afraid to hire experts. One of the biggest things that made me grow exponentially is I've worked with different consultants for 12 years. Through the networking and helping of other advisors it has made me a better entrepreneur. That's a key thing: be willing to spend a little bit of money on having consultants help you.

Susan: Build your team to strengths. You've talked about this earlier. Why don't we expand on that? How do you go about doing this?

Jon: First of all, we do specialized conative testing (striving instincts) to find out what people are really good at. I ask them, "What are you passionate about? What would you really like to do? What gives you energy when you do work?" Then we figure out as a team how that person can fit into the organization. We don't try to fit a person into a position; we try to build a position around a person.

These positions are all developing. They are all moving forward. I tell people that I want them all growing because that's where the synergy comes into play and people get excited because they know they have opportunity.

Susan: They have the freedom to know they can evolve and shape their own future. That's what allows you, Jon, to sit back and watch them create such great results.

Jon: Exactly, they are bought in. Again, it's the same thing. One out of five people, not everybody, buys into what we do, but we find the ones who do and they thrive.

Also, my most important leadership role is defining the management team. My managers will figure out the rest. I pretty much hire the advisors we are bringing on board and continue to build the management team. I have a lot of experience in managing managers. My management team is hiring and training at the staff level, and I'm hiring and training at the management level.

Susan: Good, yes, very good. That is a very helpful distinction. What would you like to share with us about training and job descriptions?

Jon: My team is big on documenting. Me, not so much, but I know it's important. We are documenting how we train people, and we've developed job descriptions for everybody in the office and that's been very helpful.

The details of job descriptions and training is more my team, and I empower them. I just oversee it. Again, I'm building the team from the management team up and advisors. My management team is taking care of the rest.

Susan: I got it. Someone's got to do the training and the job descriptions but it doesn't have to be you.

Jon: That's right.

Susan: It shouldn't be you.

Jon: It's not going to be me. It won't happen. No way, but I do know it's important.

Why Tracking Profit and Loss Is Key to Knowing What Adjustments to Make

Susan: What can you share regarding tracking profit and loss?

Jon: I enjoy managing profit and loss. I have five locations and I have five profit centers. The collection of data for my P&L is done by my management team.

I analyze my profit and loss because you need to make business decisions on whether or not you want to keep doing what you're doing or what adjustments you need to make. I spend about four to five hours a month on profit and loss and I know my business net worth.

It used to be I was only measuring profit and loss for two locations. Now it's five. If it gets much bigger we'll have to develop different infrastructure to be able to handle it.

Once a month my management team and I review profit and loss of every location and determine what direction we want to take for improving the business.

Susan: If you want five times more growth you are going to have to track your P & L or you are not going to get there.

Jon: Yes, and we have very good tracking systems.

How to Focus on What's Most Important

	Urgent	Not Urgent
Important	**I** (MANAGE) • Crisis • Medical emergencies • Pressing problems • Deadline-driven projects • Last-minute preparations for scheduled activities Quadrant of Necessity	**II** (FOCUS) • Preparation/planning • Prevention • Values clarification • Exercise • Relationship-building • True recreation/relaxation Quadrant of Quality & Personal Leadership
Not Important	**III** (AVOID) • Interruptions, some calls • Some mail & reports • Some meetings • Many "pressing" matters • Many popular activities Quadrant of Deception	**IV** (AVOID) • Trivia, busywork • Junk mail • Some phone messages/email • Time wasters • Escape activities • Viewing mindless TV shows Quadrant of Waste

Jon: One of the things that helps us to be very efficient is how we define tasks. We define tasks through the concept that was developed by Stephen Covey, and it has to do with tasks themselves. If you look at the Steven Covey matrix, he defines tasks as Important and Not Important, Urgent and Not Urgent. A task that is important and urgent is very easy to do, and almost everybody does those tasks immediately. Then you have tasks that are unimportant and urgent. You definitely shouldn't do those, because if it's unimportant, even though you think it's urgent, you shouldn't do it. Then there's unimportant and not urgent, and you should ignore those. Half of the tasks get eliminated in the matrix. Probably the most important part of the matrix is the task that is important but not urgent. People have a tendency to procrastinate and the work gets pushed out. These are B tasks as opposed to an A task, which is urgent.

What we do by tracking projects is make sure we discuss them periodically and get some kind of effort done. You're always queuing the B tasks in, even if they're not urgent. It helps to effectively manage the practice and help the team to be much more efficient.

Susan: Very good. The unimportant tasks that are tossed away, do you mean you reassign them to someone else on your team?

Jon: No, you get rid of them. If they are truly unimportant that means they're not important. You might reassign a B task that's important and not urgent, but unimportant tasks, whether they're urgent or not urgent, have no place in business, because all they do is pile up meaningless tasks that you shouldn't do.

It's very important to get rid of them, because it gets rid of intellectual clutter.

Susan: Be careful of the important but non-urgent tasks because they'll get pushed to the side by the more urgent, important and unimportant things?

Jon: Tasks that are important and not urgent tend to get pushed out. They're the hardest things to manage and one of the most important things you can manage in a business. We have systems to manage that part of it. I've always been very diligent about this in my business.

Susan: Can you give an example of something that is important but not urgent?

Jon: The perfect example is writing this book: important, not urgent. You have to queue it in. It's easy to push it off to the side. Instead, do one action. Spend five minutes on it. Don't think it's a huge task and you have to start it and complete it all at once. Pick at it. That's why I have no problem as we go through this process, and it takes four weeks, six weeks, whatever; it's going to be done right. That's an important but not urgent task.

Susan: Very well said, Jon.

Jon: I don't track most urgent and important tasks. I know they're going to get done. I do track important, not urgent tasks, because I know if you don't pay attention they won't get done.

Susan: On that matrix you really just focus on important not urgent then?

Jon: I do. I'm very good at taking the complex and simplifying it. This is how to simplify one's workload; it takes all the confusion out of it.

Susan: Agreed; it does. Any time management tips for the advisors?

Jon: You have to be disciplined. You need to empower your staff; to delegate properly and to not hold onto things because you think you're the best at it. You have to explore the emotional part of what gets in your way.

That's hard. You have to have conversations with people and ask, "Why do you hold onto that task? Why is it a high priority to keep it?" You'll find out, quite often, it's just control issues.

Susan: I suppose if you're only going to work 20 to 25 hours a week, you can't let your time be spent handling a bunch of non-critical tasks.

Jon: It actually is easy, because everybody else is doing the work. I actually sometimes run out of work to do then I do my staff a favor and I go home.

Susan: I love it.

Jon: I've been doing it this way for probably four or five years, and it's getting better, because I let go of more things. I do this because if I'm not here tomorrow, how would I want things to operate? Let's be honest, there are times when I'm stressed or I get high intensity levels of work because people are coming at me, but most of the time my staff solves it themselves. They know how to. I've empowered them to solve issues. They only bring me in when it really needs my attention. Sometimes I have to be careful of over delegating and making sure they know that I'm available to them. That is important to me, so I pay attention to that, too.

How to Build a Bigger Future

Susan: Very good Jon. What advice do you have for the advisors for not getting discouraged?

Jon: We have an attitude of keep it going. Keeping it going is really what our Thursday meetings are all about. We are always asking ourselves what's new out there. What do we want to do strategically?

Susan: How far out do you look?

Jon: 25 years.

Susan: Wow, have you looked that far out for your business?

Jon: Yes and what it does is it creates a different mindset. I just did an exercise looking out 25 years. It feels crazy looking forward 25 years but what it does is it makes you think differently. I have a thousand clients right now; projected out twenty five years that would be 10,000 clients. I have six advisors. Okay, 25 years from now I've got 100 advisors. It doesn't mean I'm necessarily going to get there but it changes my thinking.

One of the great things looking out 25 years does is teach you to be efficient because if you want to be five times bigger *and* work half the time you have to take on projects that are really meaningful and eliminate the rest. You have to be very selective. Less is more to have a lot more.

Susan: Interesting. Can you share an example with us?

Jon: Three years ago I was looking to buy any practice I came across. Now I'm being really selective and I'm purchasing better practices. If you are focused on the best match for your situation, you will be much more successful than trying to make every situation happen.

We do this with clients, too. We are selective with clients in that we always have to be moving up market and trying to make sure clients match our modeling. Being very selective allows for exponential growth.

Susan: It's a little counterintuitive. This is not just quick go find a practice and snatch it up because if it's not a fit, the amount of effort, time, energy, staff all of it can be very draining as opposed to being a profitable move for you.

Jon: Correct. We are very selective but at the same time we are aggressive in seeking opportunity. We are selective in who we choose and we tell people that. It's funny. People become more attracted to you when you do this.

Susan: You date a lot but you don't always put a ring on it.

Jon: That's an excellent point. That's what I tell people. We are dating. We are not yet married.

Susan: You have to change your thinking and approach to get five times more growth without five times more effort.

Jon: Less is more.

How to Empower Your Team to Excellence

Susan: What's the next key towards an advisor making more while working less?

Jon: A big part of our success is wanting my team to be rewarded well for what they do. Part of that reward is they build equity. What I'm doing with my team is giving them an opportunity 10 to 15 years from now by building equity; they will be buying parts of my practice while I'm still in it.

I want my business to have legacy ownership. To accomplish this, the team needs to have equity. It's about having a greater impact, generating more abundance, and rewarding my team.

Susan: Are you saying you are selling equity shares of your business to your team?

Jon: Yes, I'm going to be selling off pieces of my business when it makes business sense. I'm independently wealthy. It's not about me getting richer. It's about the team. I can't put it any other way.

Susan: I love it.

Jon: It's a little bit different for sure.

Susan: If someone has questions Jon, how can they get in touch with you?

Jon: They can call me at 607-321-2501. I like helping people. If somebody just wants to have a chat they can give me a call. I'm not looking to be a consultant. I'm looking to build my team and pass on what we do to more and more advisors.

Susan: I can imagine this is the starting point for someone who is looking to revamp their business. This highlights different areas where possibly they aren't thinking differently enough. You've shown them how they can grow their business by working a lot smarter. I want to thank you.

Jon: Thank you, too. It was a lot of fun.

Here's How to Leverage Your Team and Work Less

You already know how to be a successful financial advisor. The confusing part is knowing how to grow your business by working less, not more.

That's where we come in. We help people just like you leverage your team and time to grow your business 5x.

Step 1: We invest time getting to know each other to see if we share common goals and values.

Step 2: We help you determine if our team can help you and your practice.

Step 3: We see if we can work together using a proven system to integrate concepts, with client and advisor satisfaction as our top priorities.

Most advisors think it takes years and years of hard work and seeing client after client to grow their practice.

Now you can multiply your results 5x while working half the time.

About the Author

Jon Myers, CFP®, MBA, ChFC®, CLTC, CASL®, is a financial advisor in Vestal, New York. He has 5 offices across upstate New York. His practice manages over $300 million and works directly with over 1,000 clients. Prior to becoming a financial advisor, Jon was a program manager for a large government contractor. As a program manager, Jon oversaw a $20 million annual budget and was responsible for cost and schedule of many programs. In the early 1990s, Jon, with the help of his wife, made the decision to become a financial advisor. In his 22 years in the business, Jon has risen to be in the top 1% of producers at his broker-dealer. His recent practice growth has been fueled by the purchase of 5 other practices and the recruitment of several advisors. Jon is a strong leader of his team of 14.